MY BEST POEMS

Part 1

Celebrating

NATURE

Dramatic,
Enchanting,
Rejuvenating

© 2017 by Pia Horan-Gross

All rights reserved. No portion of this book may be reproduced, stored in a retrieval system, or transmitted in any form or by any means – electronic, mechanical, photocopy, recording, scanning, or other – except for brief quotations in critical reviews or articles, without the prior written permission of the author/self-publisher.

Unless otherwise noted, Scripture quotations are taken form the Holy Bible, New King James Version (NKJV)®. Copyright © 1982 by Thomas Nelson. Used by permission. All rights reserved.

ISBN 978-0-6480135-1-8

Table of Contents

FOREWORD	vii
A RARE VISITOR	1
AUTUMN	3
BUSY AS A BEE?	6
CELEBRATION OF LIGHT	8
EVENING DANCE	10
FIREFLIES	12
GREY SUMMER'S DAY	15
MERE WATCHING	16
MORE RAIN AHEAD	18
POETRY AGAIN	19
PREHISTORIC ERUPTION	20
SOUL BREATHING	22
SPRING MORNING	23
THE BUMBLING BUMBLE BEE	25
THE PERFECTION OF SILENCE	27
THE WALL OF STONES	28
AUTUMN LEAVES	33
BUTTERFLY	34
COALCLIFF	35
FREESIA	36
NATIVE ROSE	37

THE LOST HAT	38
THE SINGING OF THE SAW	39
THIS EARTH	41
TURTLE TIME	42
WICKETTY WAR CREEK	43

FOREWORD

*"But ask the animals, and they will teach you,
or the birds in the sky, and they will tell you;
or speak to the earth, and it will teach you,
or let the fish in the sea inform you.
Which of all these does not know
that the hand of the LORD has done this?
In his hand is the life of every creature
and the breath of all mankind."*
Job 12:7-10

From a very young age, I developed a special love and sensitivity to the natural world around me. As a five year old, I would eagerly seek out seasonal flowers and fruit, growing all around me, some in secluded, hidden places, in forests and fields, near singing creeks. They were a special delight to me. For six years, I lived in a tiny Swiss village called Seseglio, near the Italian border. For many years after, having moved away from that area, I pined for those memories.

For a long time, I was convinced that peace could only be found by seeking out nature. This proved in part true and nature continues to have a soothing influence upon me. I believe this applies to you also my reader, or you would not have chosen this book.

Only since discovering or literally stumbling over nature's Maker (sorry, not Mother Nature), nature has taken on a transcendental quality and role for me and contemplation of nature now equates to contemplation of its Maker. I often marvel at the abounding generosity of God, his humour and love of creativity, when I look at some of his quirky creative expressions, and at his goodness; as one minister would exclaim: "God is good because he created mangoes!"- and so much more! Finally, nature like mankind has become marred since its original conception and it is easy to lose sight of the inherent perfection in nature. Has it all become uncontrollable? To some extent yes, but not irreparably so.

That is my unshakable hope and belief; based on trustworthy promises, made by One who set all this in motion, a very long time ago, but not so long as to eclipse his origin and our destiny: eternity! That is his call for us and creation itself!

I have sought to introduce a fellow poet, Ron Horan, whose love for nature and poetry has always touched me deeply. He has an indisputable God-given gift, in his perception, expression and love of nature. He is what I call a true blue Aussie. He chooses the rhyming medium in his poetic expression. This publication may spur him on to finally publish his beautiful poetry!

P.H.-G.

A RARE VISITOR

Today,
I heard that sound again:
Currawong call,
Magpie chatter,
Kookaburra laughter–
all in one!

Once again,
our timid visitor
paying us a rare visit.
A privilege indeed!
Its timing–
a mystery!

Pia Horan-Gross

That long draping tail
spotted first.
Its plumage-
difficult to see in the scrub.
What the Lyrebird lacks in glamour,
it makes up in its vocal artistry.

2 November 2007

AUTUMN

Pia Horan-Gross

A rising southerly
chases reluctant clouds
across a restless sky.
The warmth and brilliance of sunlight alternate
with the coolness and dullness
of a cloudy day.

Intermittently,
wind gusts in the trees,
the lonely call of a Currawong,
followed by sudden chirping of a late cricket.
In the distance,
the voice of laughing children.

After each wind burst,
the rustling of falling leaves
spiraling to earth, outside my window.
Rainbow coloured ones,
touched by a playful artist's palette,
others in many shades of brown.

Initially,
all green and tender,
holding the same promise.
Too soon,
some withered and died.
No sap, no life.

One last attempt by the sun rays
to pierce through the dense curtain of clouds.
Once more, the world comes alive
in a symphony of colours.
My room is bathed in light.
In one accord, the crickets start singing again.

As suddenly as it appeared,
the sunlight is gone.
The crickets stop.
Nature holds its breath.
Then, the sound of isolated raindrops.
Now, the steady drumming of rain.

6 April 1988

BUSY AS A BEE?

Seated at my usual breakfast spot,
in this place of rest and beauty,
looking out
at the flowering shrub
full of industrious bees,
I spot my favourite:
the round bumble bee!
Busy bees.

When I look again,
my bumble bee
is acting
somewhat out of sync.
Not so much interested
in flowers and their scent
but rather in leaves!?
Busy bee…?

Wholly focused on a leaf,
right in front of me;
is it exploring it?
Or maybe grooming itself?
Possibly suffering from stress?
Presently, it makes its way
underneath the leaf–
"Busy as a bee?"

That's where it attaches itself and,
after some wriggling,
remains perfectly still.
I finish my breakfast–
it's still there.
Then go about some mundane tasks-
and find it's still there.
Resting bee.

A brief conversation
takes my focus off the bee.
When I look again–
it is gone!
Showing
that even bees know
when it is time to stop!
Busy, yet wise as a bee!

Seaview Farm
St. Marys, Tasmania
17 February 2007

Pia Horan-Gross

CELEBRATION OF LIGHT

Sunlight on water,
alternating with shade
from ancient trees.
Gentle ripples on the stream,
crowned by dancing sparkles,
laughing,
celebrating the light.

Sunrays,
piercing
this dark hiding place,
glittering
through my tears,
soothing
their unwelcome profusion.

7 February 2007
Goulburn River,
Seymour, Victoria

EVENING DANCE

A lingering sunset
at eventide.
The day seems to hold its breath
as the dusk gradually descends.
Not so the sea,
with its unceasing restlessness.

On the deserted beach,
near some houses,
a little girl absorbed in her sandy play.
Presently, a big dog sits down beside her.
"You are my friend", says the girl,
dancing around him.

Away they go,
running along the water's edge,
her little nightdress fluttering in the wind.
Then they sit and watch the mighty sea.
The world is theirs;
full of wonder for those with eyes to see.

"But everything is so big and
I am so little,"
the girl seems to think.
"Let's go back where we are safe!"
She takes the big dog by the collar
and pulls him back with force.

Unbeknown to both,
in the house nearest to them,
behind concealing curtains,
stand the watchful parents,
first laughing,
now their faces glowing.

> Undated,
> possibly 1978
> (re-written 2016)

FIREFLIES

Last night,
I went for a long walk
along the Daintree Forest,
on the road to Cow Bay.

I followed the bike trail,
meandering in and out
of the luscious rain forest,
and wished I had my bike.

Driven by inner pain,
I walked and walked.
An irrational desire
to beat the imminent dusk.

At "Crocodylus", I lingered long;
a series of large cabins,
picturesquely positioned
amidst the glorious rain forest.

Inside,
basic comfort.
See-through,
cool green mesh.

A direct link
to the surrounding majesty
of an ancient remnant-
nature at its best!

I should have headed back,
after that.
Instead,
I stubbornly kept walking.

Finally,
sense prevailed.
I turned back.
The sky a crimson afterglow.

Presently,
a stone bench and table
beckoned me,
near a disused "servo".

While pondering
the "For Sale" sign,
I thoroughly enjoyed
a strengthening snack.

I knew,
I wouldn't make it back
before the descending darkness
of the impending night.

Progressively,
the rain forest became dark
and mysterious,
as I finally made my way back.

Alternating
between bicycle lane
and main road,
I hastened my step.

Pia Horan-Gross

The headlight of passing vehicles
briefly revealing
a lonely walker,
amidst the darkness.

Although now my pace was fast,
it wasn't driven by fear.
Rather, a sense of wonder
at the many noises near and far.

Suddenly,
my eye caught a spark.
It was a tiny, flickering dot,
moving to and fro.

Then, nearby,
at the edge of the rain forest,
a second one–
only those two.

I felt the same delight
of so many years ago when,
as a child, I would run after them–
fireflies!

I stood transfixed,
rewarded for lingering;
the dark forest revealing
one of its nocturnal wonders!

Cow Bay, Queensland
9 October 2006

GREY SUMMER'S DAY

Funny how,
when the sky clouds over,
things revive in the garden.
Especially
near the storm water creek.
I hear the noisy, crashing sound
of a Lace Monitor passing through.
Imposing, prehistoric
seemingly slow and clumsy.
Yet, when with curiosity approached,
it heads for the nearest tree,
fast as lightening
and perfectly camouflaged!
Stay away sun,
just a little longer,
before your thirsty rays
dry up the creek once more
and shy monitor retreats deeper
into the bushland scrub!

5 February 2014

MERE WATCHING

Watching...
pen in hand, a cuppa by my side;
the water's playful ripple
driven by a gusty wind,
singing and rattling
around my little caravan.

Watching...
a silent pelican
calmly floating across the channel,
heading to its evening nesting ground.
With perfect grace and dignity,
it knows no haste nor tardiness.

Watching...
a continuous stream of cars
crossing the bridge to my right.
Opposite, the busyness of people-
shopping, working- doing.
Forgetting about the 'being'?

Watching...
the veiled yet blazing sunset-
a diva making her flamboyant exit,
surrounded by a spectacular entourage;
sombre, billowing clouds, gold edged,
on a background of vividly burnt orange.

Watching...
and exclaiming
a ridiculously inadequate "Wow!"

The silent lightening in the distance,
crowning this exuberant magnificence.
Humbled mankind- a mere spectator.

The Entrance North, New South Wales
24 October, 1999

Pia Horan-Gross

MORE RAIN AHEAD

After many days of pouring rain,
the once lazy stagnant creek-
now a rushing powerful torrent,
filling the air with an unfamiliar sound,
like a distant highway full of semi-trailers,
or the approach of a mighty storm.
Closer to home-
the drip drop outside
from leaking gutters
and the random bell sounds
from chimes on the veranda,
stroked by capricious wind gusts.
Now, the rising and falling sound
of the last autumn crickets.

My ear strains to discern
between the sound of rain
and the wind in the trees.
A falling leaf, blowing against my window
stops short my autumn reverie.
The birds have ceased their song
and silent darkness has put the day to rest.
I close the shutters of my room,
straighten my sheets and pillows
then, slowly and aching, head for the kitchen.
The comfort of the whistling kettle.
I re-arm myself with more tissues and Panadol,
sighing as I hear the latest weather update:
more rain ahead!

5 March 1995

POETRY AGAIN

I am writing poetry again, after
all this time!
The chords struck
by a strange pain,
like a haunting melody,
evoked by a time and place.
Like the memory to the palate
of wine long in the making.
Similar to a long forgotten
lingering familiar fragrance
of an expensive perfume.
Or maybe,
like discovering
glistening, colourful layers
forming the mighty rock,
brilliantly revealed after a storm.
Though not solid as rock,
rather,
elusive like morning mist,
dancing and rising in the valley,
soon making its exit.
Then,
returning again,
unexpectedly,
for a final encore.

29 April 1990

PREHISTORIC ERUPTION

A cataclysmic eruption of a volcano,
the size of a continent,
is covering a large part of the earth-
caustic dark ash
and noxious deadly fumes!

The sun, permanently eclipsed
by smoke clouds
blotting out the sky
and by rising poisonous gases,
swallowing up the whole world.

Every now and then, the misty funeral shroud
is torn open by an icy, arctic blast-
a sterile landscape is revealed.

The earth ash grey;
green breathed its last!

Black trees,
their naked limbs thrust upwards,
in dying desperation.
Nearby, the strewn, scarred remnants
of that colossi: dinosaur!

The curtains close once more.
Toxic fog takes over, darkness intensifies.
Apart from the howling storm,
no living thing moves.
Life has left for unknown millennia.

*Undated, probably late 70's,
re-written 2016*

SOUL BREATHING

Quiet houses on green hillsides.
Silent, gentle rain,
subdued cicadas
and occasional birds' twitter.
An intrusive car
soon fading in the distance.

Pale sunshine
on blades of grass.
Shiny leaves gently stirring.
Slow clouds wafting across the horizon,
torn asunder, then absorbing one another.
Grey changing to white.

Blue sky increases.
Sunlight returns
in full radiance.
The rain stops.
Resuming,
the piercing sound of cicadas.

I get up
and wonder
what to cook for dinner.

Ocean Shores, NSW
9 July 1985

SPRING MORNING

Newborn sun rays
casting long shadows across my path.
A cool breeze
swaying the gum tree hills.
Nearby, leaves gently rustling
and birds twittering.

As I cross the footbridge
over the railway line,
a crisp wind gust makes me shiver,
I pull my jacket tighter around me.
The highway below drowning out
Currawong, atop a tall Norfolk Pine.

I increase my pace
as I search for the silvery snake
in the distance.
Then I see it appear,
glistening in the morning sun.
On time!

I quickly hurry to the end of the bridge,
trot along the highway strip,
up the stairs in a puff;
the attendant ready to blow the whistle.
Last step, then I saunter through the carriage door
as the doors close –
Phew! I just made it once again!

20 October 2003

THE BUMBLING BUMBLE BEE

Today, I chose a seat
at the long rustic table,
in the cottage's shared kitchen,
to have my breakfast.
I sat near the window,
overlooking the garden.

Outside, a lilac flowering plant
with long stems,
growing up past the window sill.
Mostly leaves, the flowers small,
in the shape of bells,
sun-drenched sparkling colours!

Pia Horan-Gross

Bees, flying to and fro.
A round bumble bee,
selective in its choice of flowers,
joined the general busyness.
Its lovely shape and bright colours
filled my heart with merriment.

Aiming for the same flower,
a careless, smaller bee
made a last moment escape
from its larger counterpart.
Otherwise,
harmonious industriousness.

Suddenly, my tubby bumble bee
made an error of judgment;
it briefly attached to a flower
which could not hold its weight.
Both disappeared into the leafy undergrowth.
I laughed out loud at the jolly sight!

Then I watched anew
as the bee re-appeared,
resuming, red faced maybe?
its intensely focused labour.
No doubt,
with a little more care!

Seaview Farm, St. Marys, Tasmania
16 February 2007

THE PERFECTION OF SILENCE

Oh the bliss of wrapping myself in silence,
savouring time slowly, purposefully!
Allowing others to be,
whilst outside the ceaseless throng.

To watch birds,
riding wind currents
sculpting ripples on the water-
the ebb and flow of a tidal lagoon.

Noticing weather patterns
and their restless change.
No tecno infiltration.
No interruption to my train of thoughts.

Finally, to hum a tune,
feeling deep gratitude.
To savour, even just for a day,
the perfection of silence.

The Entrance North, New South
Wales 24 October 1999

Pia Horan-Gross

THE WALL OF STONES

I stayed in the bush,
on the Mountains called Blue.
The cottage,
touching on creative genius,
thoughtful to the needs of guests.

Love evident
for the medium used,
awakening awareness
of the unobtrusive beauty
of the Aussie bush.

Striking,
the attempt
to bring the bush inside.
Around the fireplace,
a wall built from local bush rocks.

In shape and colour,
not smooth and even
like bricks
but irregular and rustic-
each rock different.

While I breathed in stillness,
the wall began to reveal
its coded message.
Differing rocks,
yet near-perfect symmetry.

Some functional,
while others jagged
(handle with care!).
Also, big and impressive,
while still others deep and 'holey'.

Once- sunning themselves or
buried in the bush (minding their own business).
Then- discovered, picked up and scrubbed clean.
Now- purposely positioned into a feature wall.
That speaks volumes to me!

20 May 2003

Addendum

Introducing:

Poems by Ron T Horan

Contact: ***gincing2@bigpond.com***

AUTUMN LEAVES

If these autumn leaves
near the window glass
be dying leaves,
then let life pass,
for I never beheld
a more exquisite sight
in crimson dark,
or scarlet bright.

Ever perfect of colour,
never swift to fade.
Death by degree,
shade on shade.
No sudden blast
of Jack Frost breath,
just the flickering flames of
graceful death.

May 1995

BUTTERFLY

The rain has come,
the sun has gone
a butterfly its flight withdrawn
its body chilled,
its wings outspread
to lie so still-
I feared it dead.
A miracle the sunshine brings
in warmth to blood
in life to limbs
a healing force the sun imparts
to butterflies and broken hearts.

Undated

COALCLIFF

I remember Coalcliff, when Stony Creek ran
clear and clean through mother's hands
Sweet Septembers with their springtime rush
of wattle and of bottle brush

With a sense of wonder we walked down
a rough bush track wild and overgrown
with only stone for step and stair
through bracken fern and maidenhair

I remember Coalcliff, when big waves rolled
over Neptune's Rock into Mullet Hole
alchemy of salt, shell and sea
periwinkle, crab and anemone

January nights, when the moon shone true
when family sat outside, while you
counted stars, as moonlight rolled
over the ocean in waves of gold

Then the colliery came to stay
turning our shores to sands of grey
Now the ocean combers roll
not silver but black as coal

Shacks are gone, as is the track
the wild bush has claimed them back
The beauty that once was can be
now only found in memory.

Undated

FREESIA

It's springtime and every garden
is overgrown with freesia
whose errant blooms, wind sown,
find every corner, verge and nook.
Yet, to those who garden by the book,
who plant in picture perfect rows,
Begonia, Azalea, Her Lady's rose
and drape wisteria from lilac bowers-

Freesia! Do not classify as flowers,
only weeds that grow out in the street,
nod their heads to any passer-by they meet.
Freesia though, might not agree.
Despising form and symmetry,
no prisoner of garden plot-
conformity never their lot.
Rather, scale a fence, leap a border,
advancing on, in magnificent disorder.

                                          Undated

NATIVE ROSE

As red as any lover's blush
a parallel that nature chose
as fire in the springtime rush burn
the berries of the native rose. Icy
breathes a mountain wind
its breath across the saddle flows
to burn the river willows bare and
likewise burn the native rose. A
withering of sun and wind draws
every blossom to a close
a flame to light the bush afire
burns scarlet in the native rose.

Undated

THE LOST HAT

I knew not where I left it
or the last time it was seen.
I searched high and low
and everywhere in between.
In the most unlikely places
and the likely ones as well.
I even asked St. Anthony
but St. Anthony would not tell.

Then, in warm November,
I journeyed up to view
the mountains and the moon
in their springtime rendezvous
and there among the bluebells…
a hat- no longer lost
left me ruing all the worry that
losing it had cost!

September 1994

THE SINGING OF THE SAW

On the windy saddle below camp
an old grey gum
most recently felled
by some wild storm
that the night had hurled
at every root and limb
made more of a lesson
than death and decay
became an object of passion
Even love can be felt
for fallen giants
as alike is extended
for tiny trampled things.

I counted ten score
or more of rings
the growth rings of the heart
of a giant to touch the sky
From such a tiny seed does start
to grow and grow and grow.

After all the worth
of life I thought
to be more or less the same
alike for monolith or mite
and well within the orbit
of any recycled soul.

In these mountains it was winter
yet a warmer wind
told me that springtime
was not long
So with coat off
I began
to saw and saw and saw.
And I felt the blessing
and the loss
knew joy and sorrow
in the sound
heard a song as never before
in the singing of the saw.

                              Undated

THIS EARTH

This earth holds me
in its warm heat
long after the sun
to its lair retreats.

The earth bore me
from its deep bower.
From leaf, from litter,
from wild, wild, flower.

The earth awaits me
its seeds, its grasses.
Essence of existence
after existence passes.

September 1994

TURTLE TIME

Your arrival, Mister Turtle,
depends upon your gait.
When you're tardy, you are early,
when you're on time, you are late.

In slow motion every movement,
the art of stillness you remind,
of lost infinite grace
that speed has left behind.

Close your eyes now, Mister
Turtle, and breathe a grateful sigh
that this mad world rushing past
will forever pass you by.

November 1993

WICKETTY WAR CREEK

In mid-summer heat
or after fallen snow
under a scorching sun
or icicle of noon-
a starriness of stream
then a glittering of moon
call it Upper Run Creek
or the Wicketty War flow
If thoughts have a home
it's there my thoughts go
to clear, sweet water
born on Hampton High
Neither finding source
in meadow, mead or sky
To in secret, issue forth
among tussocks
lost and found
Temperance of earth
well spring unbound
beneath a river willow
over the mossy stone
through a rocky cleft
across a field new sown

down a riffle in a rush
a rapid with a roar
by she oaks with a sigh
gliding by a granite tor
till a pebbled pool
watercress and clover grass
distil the torrent thus as
translucent as glass.

"Fish River Camp"
(near Oberon, NSW)
April 1995